for

_____

from

_____

*Let us therefore come boldly to
the throne of grace, that we may
obtain mercy and find grace to
help in time of need.*

—Hebrews 4:16 (NKJV)

Authentic Publishing
We welcome your questions and comments.

USA	1820 Jet Stream Drive, Colorado Springs, CO 80921
	www.authenticbooks.com
UK	9 Holdom Avenue, Bletchley, Milton Keynes, Bucks, MK1 1QR
	www.authenticmedia.co.uk
India	Logos Bhavan, Medchal Road, Jeedimetla Village, Secunderabad 500 055, A.P.

God's Promises on Prayer
ISBN 978-1-934068-96-0

Copyright © 2008 by The Livingstone Corporation

Livingstone project staff includes Andy Culbertson, Linda Taylor, Joan Guest, Everett O'Bryan. Interior design by Lindsay Galvin and Larry Taylor.

Published in 2008 by Authentic.
All rights reserved.

A catalog record for this book is available from the Library of Congress.

Printed in the United States of America

GOD'S PROMISES

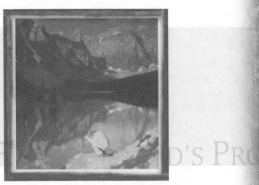

on Prayer

OD'S P   D'S PRO

CONTENTS

The Heartfelt Prayers of. . .

THE PRINCIPLES AND PROMISES OF

Prayer

*In [Christ Jesus our Lord] we
have boldness and access with
confidence through faith in Him.*

—Ephesians 3:12 (NKJV)

Why SHOULD WE PRAY?

Then if my people who are called by my name will humble themselves and pray and seek my face and turn from their wicked ways, I will hear from heaven and will forgive their sins and restore their land.

—*2 Chronicles 7:14 (NLT)*

Don't worry about anything. But pray and ask God for everything you need. And when you pray, always give thanks. And God's peace will keep your hearts and minds in Christ Jesus. That peace which God gives is so great that we cannot understand it.

—*Philippians 4:6–7 (ERV)*

Is any one of you in trouble? He should pray. Is anyone happy? Let him sing songs of praise. Is any one of you sick? He should call the elders of the church to pray over him and anoint him with oil in the name of the Lord. And the prayer offered in faith will make the sick person well; the Lord will raise him up. If he has sinned, he will be forgiven. Therefore confess your sins to each other and pray for each other so that you may be healed. The prayer of a righteous man is powerful and effective.
—*James 5:13–16 (NIV)*

He will listen to the prayers of the destitute. He will not reject their pleas. Let this be recorded for future generations, so that a people not yet born will praise the LORD.
—*Psalm 102:17–18 (NLT)*

Watch and pray, lest you enter into temptation. The spirit indeed is willing, but the flesh is weak.

—Matthew 26:41 (NKJV)

If you believe, you will receive whatever you ask for in prayer.

—Matthew 21:22 (NIV)

Keep alert at all times. And pray that you might be strong enough to escape these coming horrors and stand before the Son of Man.

—Luke 21:36 (NLT)

But if we confess (admit) our sins, then God will forgive our sins. We can trust God to do this. God does what is right. God will make us clean from all the wrong things we have done.

—1 John 1:9 (ERV)

May the words of my mouth and the meditation of my heart be pleasing in your sight, O LORD, my Rock and my Redeemer.

—*Psalm 19:14 (NIV)*

Who can go up the Lord's mountain? Who can stand and worship in the Lord's holy temple? People who have not done evil things, people who have pure hearts, people who have not used my name to make lies sound like the truth, and people who have not lied and made false promises. Only those people can worship there.

—*Psalm 24:3–4 (ERV)*

In him and through faith in him we may approach God with freedom and confidence.

—Ephesians 3:12 (NIV)

One time Jesus was praying in a place. When Jesus finished praying, one of his followers said to him, "John taught his followers how to pray. Lord, teach us how to pray too."

Jesus said to the followers, "When you pray, pray like this: 'Father, we pray that your name will always be kept holy. We pray that your kingdom will come. Give us the food we need for each day. Forgive us the sins we have done, because we forgive every person that has done wrong to us. And don't let us be tempted (tested).'"

—Luke 11:1–4 (ERV)

I have blotted out, like a thick cloud, your transgressions, and like a cloud, your sins. Return to Me, for I have redeemed you.
        —*Isaiah 44:22 (NKJV)*

Then Jesus said, "I am the bread that gives life. The person that comes to me will never be hungry. The person that believes in me will never be thirsty."
        —*John 6:35 (ERV)*

For what great nation has a god as near to them as the LORD our God is near to us whenever we call on him?
        —*Deuteronomy 4:7 (NLT)*

My little children, these things I write to you, so that you may not sin. And if anyone sins, we have an Advocate with the Father, Jesus Christ the righteous.
        —*1 John 2:1 (NKJV)*

This is the confidence we have in approaching God: that if we ask anything according to his will, he hears us.

—*1 John 5:14 (NIV)*

So you should look for the Lord before it is too late. You should call to him now, while he is near.

—*Isaiah 55:6 (ERV)*

Behold, the Lord GOD shall come with a strong hand, and His arm shall rule for Him; behold, His reward is with Him, and His work before Him. He will feed His flock like a shepherd; He will gather the lambs with His arm, and carry them in His bosom, and gently lead those who are with young.

—*Isaiah 40:10–11 (NKJV)*

Behold, I stand at the door and knock. If anyone hears My voice and opens the door, I will come in to him and dine with him, and he with Me.

—*Revelation 3:20 (NKJV)*

No one has ever seen God. But if we love each other, God lives in us, and his love is brought to full expression in us. And God has given us his Spirit as proof that we live in him and he in us. Furthermore, we have seen with our own eyes and now testify that the Father sent his Son to be the Savior of the world. All who confess that Jesus is the Son of God have God living in them, and they live in God. We know how much God loves us, and we have put our trust in his love. God is love, and all who live in love live in God, and God lives in them.

—*1 John 4:12–16 (NLT)*

I am the true grapevine, and my Father is the gardener. He cuts off every branch of mine that doesn't produce fruit, and he prunes the branches that do bear fruit so they will produce even more. You have already been pruned and purified by the message I have given you. Remain in me, and I will remain in you. For a branch cannot produce fruit if it is severed from the vine, and you cannot be fruitful unless you remain in me.

—*John 15:1–4 (NLT)*

If you remain in me and my words remain in you, ask whatever you wish, and it will be given you. This is to my Father's glory, that you bear much fruit, showing yourselves to be my disciples.

—*John 15:7–8 (NIV)*

But as for me, how good it is to be near God! I have made the Sovereign LORD my shelter, and I will tell everyone about the wonderful things you do.
—*Psalm 73:28 (NLT)*

This includes you who were once far away from God. You were his enemies, separated from him by your evil thoughts and actions. Yet now he has reconciled you to himself through the death of Christ in his physical body. As a result, he has brought you into his own presence, and you are holy and blameless as you stand before him without a single fault.
—*Colossians 1:21–22 (NLT)*

And in him you too are being built together to become a dwelling in which God lives by his Spirit.
—*Ephesians 2:22 (NIV)*

And this is His commandment: that we should believe on the name of His Son Jesus Christ and love one another, as He gave us commandment. Now he who keeps His commandments abides in Him, and He in him. And by this we know that He abides in us, by the Spirit whom He has given us.
—*1 John 3:23–24 (NKJV)*

My soul longs, yes, even faints for the courts of the LORD; my heart and my flesh cry out for the living God.
—*Psalm 84:2 (NKJV)*

You received Christ Jesus the Lord. So continue to live following him without changing anything. You must depend on Christ only. Life and strength come from him. You were taught the truth. You must continue to be sure of that true teaching. And always be thankful.
—*Colossians 2:6–7 (ERV)*

I tell you the truth, anyone who believes in me will do the same works I have done, and even greater works, because I am going to be with the Father. You can ask for anything in my name, and I will do it, so that the Son can bring glory to the Father. Yes, ask me for anything in my name, and I will do it!

—*John 14:12–14 (NLT)*

So I say to you: Ask and it will be given to you; seek and you will find; knock and the door will be opened to you. For everyone who asks receives; he who seeks finds; and to him who knocks, the door will be opened.

—*Luke 11:9–10 (NIV)*

In him and through faith in him we may approach God with freedom and confidence.
—Ephesians 3:12 (NIV)

The Lord heard my prayer. And the Lord accepted and answered my prayer.
—Psalm 6:9 (ERV)

I have followed your paths. My feet never left your way of living. Every time I called to you, God, you answered me. So listen to me now. God, you help people who trust you—those people stand by your right side. So listen to this prayer from one of your followers.
—Psalm 17:5–7 (ERV)

You didn't choose me. I chose you. I appointed you to go and produce lasting fruit, so that the Father will give you whatever you ask for, using my name.
—John 15:16 (NLT)

Let us therefore come boldly to the throne of grace, that we may obtain mercy and find grace to help in time of need.

—*Hebrews 4:16 (NKJV)*

The LORD said, "I have indeed seen the misery of my people in Egypt. I have heard them crying out because of their slave drivers, and I am concerned about their suffering."

—*Exodus 3:7 (NIV)*

For the LORD your God is God of gods and Lord of lords, the great God, mighty and awesome, who shows no partiality nor takes a bribe. He administers justice for the fatherless and the widow, and loves the stranger, giving him food and clothing.

—*Deuteronomy 10:17–18 (NKJV)*

So Peter was kept in jail. But the church was constantly praying to God for Peter.

Peter was sleeping between two of the soldiers. He was bound with two chains. More soldiers were guarding the door of the jail. It was at night, and Herod planned to bring Peter out before the people the next day. Suddenly, an angel of the Lord stood there. A light shined in the room. The angel touched Peter on the side and woke him up. The angel said, "Hurry, get up!" The chains fell off Peter's hands. The angel said to Peter, "Get dressed and put on your shoes." And so Peter did this. Then the angel said, "Put on your coat and follow me." So the angel went out and Peter followed. Peter did not know if the angel was really doing this. He thought he might be seeing a vision. Peter and the angel went past the first guard and the second guard. Then they came to the iron gate that separated them from the city. The gate opened itself for them. Peter and the angel went through the gate and walked about a block. Then the angel suddenly left.

Peter realized then what had happened. He thought, "Now I know that the Lord really sent his angel to me. He rescued (saved) me from Herod. The Jewish people thought that bad things would happen to me. But the Lord saved me from all these things."

When Peter realized this, he went to the home of Mary. She was the mother of John. (John was also called Mark.) Many people were gathered there. They were all praying.

—*Acts 12:5–12 (ERV)*

But you see the trouble and grief they cause. You take note of it and punish them. The helpless put their trust in you. You defend the orphans. . . . LORD, you know the hopes of the helpless. Surely you will hear their cries and comfort them.

—*Psalm 10:14, 17 (NLT)*

The Lord protects good people. He hears their prayers.

—*Psalm 34:15 (ERV)*

I will answer them before they even call to me. While they are still talking about their needs, I will go ahead and answer their prayers!

—*Isaiah 65:24 (NLT)*

For he will deliver the needy who cry out, the afflicted who have no one to help.

—*Psalm 72:12 (NIV)*

Behold, the LORD's hand is not shortened, that it cannot save; nor His ear heavy, that it cannot hear.
—*Isaiah 59:1 (NKJV)*

He was the one who prayed to the God of Israel, "Oh, that you would bless me and expand my territory! Please be with me in all that I do, and keep me from all trouble and pain!" And God granted him his request.
—*1 Chronicles 4:10 (NLT)*

God made our ears, so surely he has ears too, and can hear what is happening! God made our eyes, so surely he has eyes too, and can see what is happening!
—*Psalm 94:9 (ERV)*

Those who know your name trust in you, for you, O LORD, do not abandon those who search for you.
—*Psalm 9:10 (NLT)*

Now as they went out of Jericho, a great multitude followed Him. And behold, two blind men sitting by the road, when they heard that Jesus was passing by, cried out, saying, "Have mercy on us, O Lord, Son of David!" Then the multitude warned them that they should be quiet; but they cried out all the more, saying, "Have mercy on us, O Lord, Son of David!" So Jesus stood still and called them, and said, "What do you want Me to do for you?" They said to Him, "Lord, that our eyes may be opened." So Jesus had compassion and touched their eyes. And immediately their eyes received sight, and they followed Him.

—*Matthew 20:29–34 (NKJV)*

Therefore I will look to the LORD; I will wait for the God of my salvation; My God will hear me.

—*Micah 7:7 (NKJV)*

Then Jonah prayed to the LORD his God from inside the fish. He said, "I cried out to the LORD in my great trouble, and he answered me. I called to you from the land of the dead, and LORD, you heard me! You threw me into the ocean depths, and I sank down to the heart of the sea. The mighty waters engulfed me; I was buried beneath your wild and stormy waves. Then I said, 'O LORD, you have driven me from your presence. Yet I will look once more toward your holy Temple.' I sank beneath the waves, and the waters closed over me. Seaweed wrapped itself around my head. I sank down to the very roots of the mountains. I was imprisoned in the earth, whose gates lock shut forever. But you, O LORD my God, snatched me from the jaws of death! As my life was slipping away, I remembered the LORD. And my earnest prayer went out to you in your holy Temple." . . . Then the LORD ordered the fish to spit Jonah out onto the beach.

—*Jonah 2:1–7, 10 (NLT)*

Now it happened in the process of time that the king of Egypt died. Then the children of Israel groaned because of the bondage, and they cried out; and their cry came up to God because of the bondage. So God heard their groaning, and God remembered His covenant with Abraham, with Isaac, and with Jacob. And God looked upon the children of Israel, and God acknowledged them.

—*Exodus 2:23–25 (NKJV)*

For the eyes of the LORD run to and fro throughout the whole earth, to show Himself strong on behalf of those whose heart is loyal to Him.

—*2 Chronicles 16:9 (NKJV)*

I called on Your name, O LORD, from the lowest pit. You have heard my voice: "Do not hide Your ear From my sighing, from my cry for help." You drew near on the day I called on You, and said, "Do not fear!" O Lord, You have pleaded the case for my soul; You have redeemed my life.

—*Lamentations 3:55–58 (NKJV)*

For there is no difference between Jew and Gentile—the same Lord is Lord of all and richly blesses all who call on him.

—*Romans 10:12 (NIV)*

We should hold strongly to the hope that we have. And we should never fail to tell people about our hope. We can trust God to do what he promised.

—*Hebrews 10:23 (ERV)*

Then he continued, "Do not be afraid, Daniel. Since the first day that you set your mind to gain understanding and to humble yourself before your God, your words were heard, and I have come in response to them."

—*Daniel 10:12 (NIV)*

Persistence IN PRAYER

Listen to my voice in the morning,
LORD. Each morning I bring my
requests to you and wait expectantly.
     —Psalm 5:3 (NLT)

I praise the Lord because he taught
me well. Even at night, he put his
instructions deep inside my mind. I
keep the Lord before me always. And I
will never leave his right side.
     —Psalm 16:7–8 (ERV)

Every day the Lord shows his true love
and every night, I have a song for him,
a prayer for my Living God.
     —Psalm 42:8 (ERV)

Be joyful in hope, patient in affliction,
faithful in prayer.
     —Romans 12:12 (NIV)

Let my prayer be set before You as incense, the lifting up of my hands as the evening sacrifice.
—*Psalm 141:2 (NKJV)*

As for me, I will call upon God, and the LORD shall save me. Evening and morning and at noon I will pray, and cry aloud, and He shall hear my voice.
—*Psalm 55:16–17 (NKJV)*

At midnight I rise to give you thanks for your righteous laws.
—*Psalm 119:62 (NIV)*

I want men everywhere to pray. These men who lift up their hands in prayer must be pleasing to God. They must not be men who become angry and have arguments.
—*1 Timothy 2:8 (ERV)*

Continue earnestly in prayer, being vigilant in it with thanksgiving.
—*Colossians 4:2 (NKJV)*

Yet give attention to your servant's prayer and his plea for mercy, O LORD my God. Hear the cry and the prayer that your servant is praying in your presence. May your eyes be open toward this temple day and night, this place of which you said you would put your Name there. May you hear the prayer your servant prays toward this place. Hear the supplications of your servant and of your people Israel when they pray toward this place. Hear from heaven, your dwelling place; and when you hear, forgive.

—*2 Chronicles 6:19–21 (NIV)*

Pray in the Spirit at all times and on every occasion. Stay alert and be persistent in your prayers for all believers everywhere.

—*Ephesians 6:18 (NLT)*

And when you pray, do not be like the hypocrites, for they love to pray standing in the synagogues and on the street corners to be seen by men. I tell you the truth, they have received their reward in full. But when you pray, go into your room, close the door and pray to your Father, who is unseen. Then your Father, who sees what is done in secret, will reward you.

—*Matthew 6:5–6 (NIV)*

God knows how often I pray for you. Day and night I bring you and your needs in prayer to God, whom I serve with all my heart by spreading the Good News about his Son. One of the things I always pray for is the opportunity, God willing, to come at last to see you.

—*Romans 1:9–10 (NLT)*

Timothy, I thank God for you—the God I serve with a clear conscience, just as my ancestors did. Night and day I constantly remember you in my prayers.

—*2 Timothy 1:3 (NLT)*

And I said: "I pray, LORD God of heaven, O great and awesome God, You who keep Your covenant and mercy with those who love You and observe Your commandments, please let Your ear be attentive and Your eyes open, that You may hear the prayer of Your servant which I pray before You now, day and night, for the children of Israel Your servants, and confess the sins of the children of Israel which we have sinned against You."

—*Nehemiah 1:5–6 (NKJV)*

Then Jesus told his disciples a parable to show them that they should always pray and not give up. He said: "In a certain town there was a judge who neither feared God nor cared about men. And there was a widow in that town who kept coming to him with the plea, 'Grant me justice against my adversary.' For some time he refused. But finally he said to himself, 'Even though I don't fear God or care about men, yet because this widow keeps bothering me, I will see that she gets justice, so that she won't eventually wear me out with her coming!'" And the Lord said, "Listen to what the unjust judge says. And will not God bring about justice for his chosen ones, who cry out to him day and night? Will he keep putting them off? I tell you, he will see that they get justice, and quickly.

However, when the Son of Man comes, will he find faith on the earth?"
—*Luke 18:1–8 (NIV)*

I waited patiently for the LORD; he turned to me and heard my cry.
—*Psalm 40:1 (NIV)*

We always remember you when we pray and we thank God for all of you.
—*1 Thessalonians 1:2 (ERV)*

Night and day we pray most earnestly that we may see you again and supply what is lacking in your faith.
—*1 Thessalonians 3:10 (NIV)*

Never stop praying.
—*1 Thessalonians 5:17 (NLT)*

Therefore we also pray always for you that our God would count you worthy of this calling, and fulfill all the good pleasure of His goodness and the work of faith with power.
—*2 Thessalonians 1:11 (NKJV)*

One day some parents brought their little children to Jesus so he could touch and bless them. But when the disciples saw this, they scolded the parents for bothering him. Then Jesus called for the children and said to the disciples, "Let the children come to me. Don't stop them! For the Kingdom of God belongs to those who are like these children. I tell you the truth, anyone who doesn't receive the Kingdom of God like a child will never enter it."

—Luke 18:15–17 (NLT)

My God will cast them away, because they did not obey Him; and they shall be wanderers among the nations.

—Hosea 9:17 (NKJV)

The LORD is far from the wicked, but he hears the prayers of the righteous.
—*Proverbs 15:29 (NLT)*

When you are praying, and you remember that you are angry with another person about something, then forgive that person. Forgive them so that your Father in heaven will also forgive your sins.
—*Mark 11:25 (ERV)*

Also, I tell you that if two of you on earth agree about something, then you can pray for it. And the thing you ask for will be done for you by my Father in heaven.
—*Matthew 18:19 (ERV)*

For the eyes of the Lord are on the righteous and his ears are attentive to their prayer, but the face of the Lord is against those who do evil.
—*1 Peter 3:12 (NIV)*

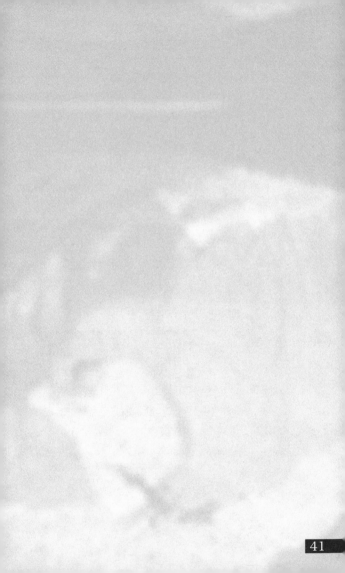

*O my Strength, to you I sing praises,
for you, O God, are my refuge, the
God who shows me unfailing love.*

—Psalm 59:17 (NLT)

Thanksgiving

Blessed be the LORD, who has given rest to His people Israel, according to all that He promised. There has not failed one word of all His good promise, which He promised through His servant Moses.

—*1 Kings 8:56 (NKJV)*

Praise the Lord! He heard my prayer for mercy.

—*Psalm 28:6 (ERV)*

Lord, you have made me very happy! I am happier now than at harvest time— when we celebrate because we have much grain and wine. I go to bed and sleep in peace. Why? Because, Lord, you lay me down to sleep in safety.

—*Psalm 4:7–8 (ERV)*

God has surely listened and heard my voice in prayer. Praise be to God, who has not rejected my prayer or withheld his love from me!

—*Psalm 66:19–20 (NIV)*

I praise the Lord with all my heart. Lord, I will tell about all the wonderful things you did. You make me so very happy. God Most-High, I praise your name. . . . You are the good judge. You sat on your throne as judge. Lord, you listened to my case. And you made the decision about me.

—*Psalm 9:1–2, 4 (ERV)*

Are any of you suffering hardships? You should pray. Are any of you happy? You should sing praises.

—*James 5:13 (NLT)*

Then they took away the stone from the place where the dead man was lying. And Jesus lifted up His eyes and said, "Father, I thank You that You have heard Me. And I know that You always hear Me, but because of the people who are standing by I said this, that they may believe that You sent Me."

—*John 11:41–42 (NKJV)*

Praise the LORD, O my soul, and forget not all his benefits—who forgives all your sins and heals all your diseases, who redeems your life from the pit and crowns you with love and compassion, who satisfies your desires with good things so that your youth is renewed like the eagle's.

—*Psalm 103:2–5 (NIV)*

I will sing to the LORD, for he has been good to me.

—*Psalm 13:6 (NIV)*

The next day Jesus went to a town called Nain. Jesus' followers and a large group of people were traveling with him. When Jesus came near the town gates, he saw a funeral. A mother, who was a widow, had lost her only son. Many people from the town were there with the mother while her son was being carried out. When the Lord (Jesus) saw her, he felt very sorry for her. Jesus said to her, "Don't cry." Jesus walked to the coffin and touched it. The men that were carrying the coffin stopped. Jesus said to the dead son, "Young man, I tell you, get up!" Then the son sat up and began to talk. Jesus gave him to his mother.

All the people were filled with fear. They began praising God and said, "A great prophet has come to us!" And they said, "God is taking care of his people."

—*Luke 7:11–16 (ERV)*

The Lord is my Rock, my Fortress, my Place of Safety. He is my God, the Rock I run to for protection. God is my shield. His power saves me. The Lord is my hiding place, my place of safety, high in the hills. He saves me from the cruel enemy. They made fun of me. But I called to the Lord for help, and I was saved from my enemies! . . . Trapped, I called to the Lord for help. Yes, I called to my God. God was in his temple. He heard my voice. He heard my cry for help.

—2 Samuel 22:2–4, 7 (ERV)

"But so that you may know that the Son of Man has authority on earth to forgive sins . . ." Then he said to the paralytic, "Get up, take your mat and go home." And the man got up and went home. When the crowd saw this, they were filled with awe; and they praised God, who had given such authority to men.

—*Matthew 9:6–8 (NIV)*

Worship AND PRAISE

Praise the LORD. Praise God in his sanctuary; praise him in his mighty heavens. Praise him for his acts of power; praise him for his surpassing greatness. Praise him with the sounding of the trumpet, praise him with the harp and lyre, praise him with tambourine and dancing, praise him with the strings and flute, praise him with the clash of cymbals, praise him with resounding cymbals. Let everything that has breath praise the LORD. Praise the LORD.

—*Psalm 150 (NIV)*

But I trust in your unfailing love. I will rejoice because you have rescued me. I will sing to the LORD because he is good to me.

—*Psalm 13:5–6 (NLT)*

Because Your lovingkindness is better than life, my lips shall praise You. Thus I will bless You while I live; I will lift up my hands in Your name. My soul shall be satisfied as with marrow and fatness, and my mouth shall praise You with joyful lips.

—*Psalm 63:3–5 (NKJV)*

The LORD is my strength and song, and He has become my salvation; He is my God, and I will praise Him; my father's God, and I will exalt Him.

—*Exodus 15:2 (NKJV)*

The next day the great crowd that had come for the Feast heard that Jesus was on his way to Jerusalem. They took palm branches and went out to meet him, shouting,

"Hosanna!"

"Blessed is he who comes in the name of the Lord!"

"Blessed is the King of Israel!"

—*John 12:12–13 (NIV)*

Jehoshaphat encouraged and instructed the people. Then he chose men to be singers to the Lord. Those singers were chosen to give praise to the Lord because he is holy and wonderful. They marched in front of the army and praised the Lord. They sang the song, Praise the Lord, because his love continues forever!

—*2 Chronicles 20:21 (ERV)*

Your righteousness is like the mighty mountains, your justice like the great deep. O LORD, you preserve both man and beast.
        —*Psalm 36:6 (NIV)*

He loves whatever is just and good; the unfailing love of the LORD fills the earth.
        —*Psalm 33:5 (NLT)*

This is how God showed his love to us: God sent his only Son into the world to give us life through him. True love is God's love for us, not our love for God. God sent his Son to be the way that God takes away our sins.
        —*1 John 4:9–10 (ERV)*

For You, Lord, are good, and ready to forgive, and abundant in mercy to all those who call upon You.
        —*Psalm 86:5 (NKJV)*

God, you are famous. People praise you everywhere on earth. Everyone knows how good you are.

—*Psalm 48:10 (ERV)*

I will give thanks to the LORD because of his righteousness and will sing praise to the name of the LORD Most High.

—*Psalm 7:17 (NIV)*

For the LORD hears the poor, and does not despise His prisoners.

—*Psalm 69:33 (NKJV)*

The LORD is gracious and full of compassion, slow to anger and great in mercy. The Lord is good to all, and His tender mercies are over all His works.

—*Psalm 145:8–9 (NKJV)*

O my Strength, to you I sing praises, for you, O God, are my refuge, the God who shows me unfailing love.

—*Psalm 59:17 (NLT)*

I will sing of your love and justice; to you, O LORD, I will sing praise.
—Psalm 101:1 (NIV)

I will proclaim the name of the LORD. Oh, praise the greatness of our God! He is the Rock, his works are perfect, and all his ways are just. A faithful God who does no wrong, upright and just is he.
—Deuteronomy 32:3–4 (NIV)

God, your kindness makes me very happy. You have seen my suffering. You know about the troubles I have.
—Psalm 31:7 (ERV)

The LORD lives! Blessed be my Rock! Let God be exalted, the Rock of my salvation!
—2 Samuel 22:47 (NKJV)

Accept, O LORD, the willing praise of my mouth, and teach me your laws.
—Psalm 119:108 (NIV)

The LORD lives! Praise to my Rock! May the God of my salvation be exalted!
—*Psalm 18:46 (NLT)*

I prayed and you helped me! You changed my crying into dancing. You took away my clothes of sadness. And you wrapped me in happiness. Lord, my God, I will praise you forever, so there will never be silence, and there will always be someone singing songs to honor you.
—*Psalm 30:11–12 (ERV)*

In that day you will say: "Give thanks to the LORD, call on his name; make known among the nations what he has done, and proclaim that his name is exalted. Sing to the LORD, for he has done glorious things; let this be known to all the world."
—*Isaiah 12:4–5 (NIV)*

Then, as He was now drawing near the descent of the Mount of Olives, the whole multitude of the disciples began to rejoice and praise God with a loud voice for all the mighty works they had seen, saying: "'Blessed is the King who comes in the name of the LORD!' Peace in heaven and glory in the highest!"
—*Luke 19:37–38 (NKJV)*

God has spoken plainly, and I have heard it many times: Power, O God, belongs to you; unfailing love, O Lord, is yours. Surely you repay all people according to what they have done.
—*Psalm 62:11–12 (NLT)*

For who is God except the LORD? Who but our God is a solid rock? God arms me with strength, and he makes my way perfect.
—*Psalm 18:31–32 (NLT)*

Praise Him, sun and moon; praise Him, all you stars of light! Praise Him, you heavens of heavens, and you waters above the heavens! Let them praise the name of the LORD, for He commanded and they were created. He also established them forever and ever; He made a decree which shall not pass away. Praise the LORD from the earth, you great sea creatures and all the depths; fire and hail, snow and clouds; stormy wind, fulfilling His word; mountains and all hills; fruitful trees and all cedars; beasts and all cattle; creeping things and flying fowl.

—*Psalm 148:3–10 (NKJV)*

You are God! Lord, only you are God! You made the sky! You made the highest heavens, and everything in them! You made the earth, and everything on it! You made the seas, and everything in them! You give life to everything! And all the heavenly angels bow down and worship you!
 —*Nehemiah 9:6 (ERV)*

Let all that I am praise the LORD. O LORD my God, how great you are! You are robed with honor and majesty. You are dressed in a robe of light. You stretch out the starry curtain of the heavens; you lay out the rafters of your home in the rain clouds. You make the clouds your chariot; you ride upon the wings of the wind. The winds are your messengers; flames of fire are your servants.
 —*Psalm 104:1–4 (NLT)*

Give to the LORD the glory he deserves!
Bring your offering and come into his
presence. Worship the LORD in all his
holy splendor. Let all the earth tremble
before him. The world stands firm and
cannot be shaken. Let the heavens
be glad, and the earth rejoice! Tell all
the nations, "The LORD reigns!" Let
the sea and everything in it shout his
praise! Let the fields and their crops
burst out with joy! Let the trees of the
forest rustle with praise, for the LORD is
coming to judge the earth. Give thanks
to the LORD, for he is good! His faithful
love endures forever.

—*1 Chronicles 16:29–34 (NLT)*

Comfort AND PEACE

But now, O Jacob, listen to the LORD
who created you. O Israel, the one who
formed you says, "Do not be afraid,
for I have ransomed you. I have called
you by name; you are mine. When you
go through deep waters, I will be with
you. When you go through rivers of
difficulty, you will not drown. When you
walk through the fire of oppression, you
will not be burned up; the flames will
not consume you. For I am the LORD,
your God, the Holy One of Israel, your
Savior. I gave Egypt as a ransom for
your freedom; I gave Ethiopia and Seba
in your place."

—Isaiah 43:1–3 (NLT)

As one whom his mother comforts, so I will comfort you; and you shall be comforted in Jerusalem.

—*Isaiah 66:13 (NKJV)*

Even though I walk through the valley of the shadow of death, I will fear no evil, for you are with me; your rod and your staff, they comfort me.

—*Psalm 23:4 (NIV)*

Heavens and Earth, be happy! Mountains, shout with joy! Why? Because the Lord comforts his people. The Lord is good to his poor people.

—*Isaiah 49:13 (ERV)*

Send me a sign of your favor. Then those who hate me will be put to shame, for you, O LORD, help and comfort me.

—*Psalm 86:17 (NLT)*

Be my rock of refuge, to which I can always go; give the command to save me, for you are my rock and my fortress.

—Psalm 71:3 (NIV)

The high and lofty one who lives in eternity, the Holy One, says this: "I live in the high and holy place with those whose spirits are contrite and humble. I restore the crushed spirit of the humble and revive the courage of those with repentant hearts."

—Isaiah 57:15 (NLT)

As the deer pants for streams of water, so my soul pants for you, O God. My soul thirsts for God, for the living God. When can I go and meet with God?

—Psalm 42:1–2 (NIV)

Give all your worries and cares to God, for he cares about you.

—1 Peter 5:7 (NLT)

Praise be to the God and Father of our Lord Jesus Christ. God is the Father who is full of mercy. He is the God of all comfort. He comforts us every time we have trouble, so that we can comfort other people any time they have trouble. We can comfort them with the same comfort that God gives us.

—*2 Corinthians 1:3–4 (ERV)*

Lord, see my suffering and rescue me. I have not forgotten your teachings.

—*Psalm 119:153 (ERV)*

From the end of the earth I will cry to You, when my heart is overwhelmed; lead me to the rock that is higher than I. For You have been a shelter for me, a strong tower from the enemy.

—*Psalm 61:2–3 (NKJV)*

I remembered Your judgments of old, O LORD, and have comforted myself.

—*Psalm 119:52 (NKJV)*

Do not be anxious about anything, but in everything, by prayer and petition, with thanksgiving, present your requests to God. And the peace of God, which transcends all understanding, will guard your hearts and your minds in Christ Jesus.

—*Philippians 4:6–7 (NIV)*

Let the peace of Christ rule in your hearts, since as members of one body you were called to peace. And be thankful.

—*Colossians 3:15 (NIV)*

Come to Me, all you who labor and are heavy laden, and I will give you rest.

—*Matthew 11:28 (NKJV)*

I sought the LORD, and he answered me; he delivered me from all my fears.

—*Psalm 34:4 (NIV)*

The Lord is close to every person who calls to him for help. The Lord is close to every person who truly worships him.

> —*Psalm 145:18 (ERV)*

I am leaving you with a gift—peace of mind and heart. And the peace I give is a gift the world cannot give. So don't be troubled or afraid.

> —*John 14:27 (NLT)*

The LORD is my shepherd, I shall not be in want. He makes me lie down in green pastures, he leads me beside quiet waters, he restores my soul. He guides me in paths of righteousness for his name's sake.

> —*Psalm 23:1–3 (NIV)*

Truly my soul silently waits for God; from Him comes my salvation.

> —*Psalm 62:1 (NKJV)*

Show us your unfailing love, O LORD,
and grant us your salvation.
—*Psalm 85:7 (NIV)*

While Christ lived on earth he prayed
to God and asked God for help. God
is the One who could save him from
death, and Jesus prayed to God with
loud cries and tears. And God answered
Jesus' prayers because Jesus was
humble and did everything God wanted.
Jesus was the Son of God. But Jesus
suffered and learned to obey by the
things that he suffered. Then Jesus was
perfect. And Jesus is the reason that
all those people who obey him can have
salvation forever.
—*Hebrews 5:7–9 (ERV)*

But you, dear friends, must build
each other up in your most holy faith,
pray in the power of the Holy Spirit,
and await the mercy of our Lord Jesus
Christ, who will bring you eternal life.
In this way, you will keep yourselves
safe in God's love.

—Jude 20–21 (NLT)

Every person that sees the Son and
believes in him has life forever. I will
raise up that person on the last day.
This is what my Father wants.

—John 6:40 (ERV)

Most assuredly, I say to you, he who
hears My word and believes in Him
who sent Me has everlasting life, and
shall not come into judgment, but has
passed from death into life.

—John 5:24 (NKJV)

A man came to Jesus and asked, "Teacher, what good thing must I do to have life forever?"

Jesus answered, "Why do you ask me about what is good? Only God is good. But if you want to have life forever, obey the commands."

The man asked, "Which commands?"

Jesus answered, "'You must not murder anyone, you must not do the sin of adultery, you must not steal anything, you must not tell lies about other people, you must honor (respect) your father and mother,' and 'you must love other people the same as you love yourself.'"

The young man said, "I have obeyed all these things. What else do I need?"

Jesus answered, "If you want to be perfect, then go and sell all the things you own. Give the money to the poor people. If you do this, you will have a

rich treasure in heaven. Then come and
follow me!"
—*Matthew 19:16–21 (ERV)*

For God loved the world so much that
he gave his one and only Son, so that
everyone who believes in him will not
perish but have eternal life.
—*John 3:16 (NLT)*

My sheep listen to my voice; I know
them, and they follow me. I give them
eternal life, and they will never perish.
No one can snatch them away from me.
—*John 10:27–28 (NLT)*

Whoever drinks the water I give him
will never thirst. Indeed, the water I
give him will become in him a spring of
water welling up to eternal life.
—*John 4:14 (NIV)*

Then a teacher of the law stood up. He was trying to test Jesus. He said, "Teacher, what must I do to get life forever?"

Jesus said to him, "What is written in the law? What do you understand from it?"

The man answered, "'You must love the Lord your God. You must love him with all your heart, all your soul, all your strength, and all your mind.' Also, 'You must love other people the same as you love yourself.'"

Jesus said to him, "Your answer is right. Do this and you will have life forever."

—*Luke 10:25–28 (ERV)*

If you confess with your mouth the Lord Jesus and believe in your heart that God has raised Him from the dead, you will be saved.

—*Romans 10:9 (NKJV)*

And this is the testimony: that God has given us eternal life, and this life is in His Son. He who has the Son has life; he who does not have the Son of God does not have life. These things I have written to you who believe in the name of the Son of God, that you may know that you have eternal life, and that you may continue to believe in the name of the Son of God. Now this is the confidence that we have in Him, that if we ask anything according to His will, He hears us. And if we know that He hears us, whatever we ask, we know that we have the petitions that we have asked of Him.

—*1 John 5:11–15 (NKJV)*

After this prayer, the meeting place shook, and they were all filled with the Holy Spirit. Then they preached the word of God with boldness.

—*Acts 4:31 (NLT)*

Peter said to them, "Change your hearts and lives and be baptized, each one of you, in the name of Jesus Christ. Then God will forgive your sins, and you will receive the gift of the Holy Spirit."

—*Acts 2:38 (ERV)*

So I say to you: Ask and it will be given to you; seek and you will find; knock and the door will be opened to you. For everyone who asks receives; he who seeks finds; and to him who knocks, the door will be opened. Which of you fathers, if your son asks for a fish, will give him a snake instead? Or if he asks for an egg, will give him a scorpion? If you then, though you are evil, know how to give good gifts to your children, how much more will your Father in heaven give the Holy Spirit to those who ask him!

—*Luke 11:9–13 (NIV)*

Now may the God of hope fill you with all joy and peace in believing, that you may abound in hope by the power of the Holy Spirit.

—Romans 15:13 (NKJV)

Now when the apostles who were at Jerusalem heard that Samaria had received the word of God, they sent Peter and John to them, who, when they had come down, prayed for them that they might receive the Holy Spirit. For as yet He had fallen upon none of them. They had only been baptized in the name of the Lord Jesus. Then they laid hands on them, and they received the Holy Spirit.

—Acts 8:14–17 (NKJV)

If you love me, obey my commandments. And I will ask the Father, and he will give you another Advocate, who will never leave you. He is the Holy Spirit, who leads into all truth. The world cannot receive him, because it isn't looking for him and doesn't recognize him. But you know him, because he lives with you now and later will be in you.
—*John 14:15–17 (NLT)*

In the same way, the Spirit helps us in our weakness. We do not know what we ought to pray for, but the Spirit himself intercedes for us with groans that words cannot express.
—*Romans 8:26 (NIV)*

And in Christ you people are being built together with the other people (the Jews). You are being made into a place where God lives through the Spirit.
—*Ephesians 2:22 (ERV)*

And it happened, while Apollos was at Corinth, that Paul, having passed through the upper regions, came to Ephesus. And finding some disciples he said to them, "Did you receive the Holy Spirit when you believed?" So they said to him, "We have not so much as heard whether there is a Holy Spirit." And he said to them, "Into what then were you baptized?" So they said, "Into John's baptism." Then Paul said, "John indeed baptized with a baptism of repentance, saying to the people that they should believe on Him who would come after him, that is, on Christ Jesus." When they heard this, they were baptized in the name of the Lord Jesus. And when Paul had laid hands on them, the Holy Spirit came upon them, and they spoke with tongues and prophesied.

—*Acts 19:1–6 (NKJV)*

Then Jesus said again, "Peace be with you! The Father sent me. In the same way, I now send you." After Jesus said that, he breathed on the followers. Jesus said, "Receive the Holy Spirit."
—*John 20:21–22 (ERV)*

Forgiveness

Have mercy upon me, O God, according to Your lovingkindness; according to the multitude of Your tender mercies, blot out my transgressions.

—*Psalm 51:1 (NKJV)*

May you hear the humble and earnest requests from me and your people Israel when we pray toward this place. Yes, hear us from heaven where you live, and when you hear, forgive.

—*2 Chronicles 6:21 (NLT)*

Who can discern his errors? Forgive my hidden faults. Keep your servant also from willful sins; may they not rule over me. Then will I be blameless, innocent of great transgression.

—*Psalm 19:12–13 (NIV)*

If you return to the Almighty, you will be built up; you will remove iniquity far from your tents. . . . For then you will have your delight in the Almighty, and lift up your face to God. You will make your prayer to Him, He will hear you, and you will pay your vows.

—*Job 22:23, 26–27 (NKJV)*

For if you forgive men their trespasses, your heavenly Father will also forgive you. But if you do not forgive men their trespasses, neither will your Father forgive your trespasses.

—*Matthew 6:14–15 (NKJV)*

Indeed it was for my own peace that I had great bitterness; but You have lovingly delivered my soul from the pit of corruption, for You have cast all my sins behind Your back.

—*Isaiah 38:17 (NKJV)*

Health AND HEALING

Lord, if you heal me, I truly will be healed. Save me, and I truly will be saved. Lord, I praise you!
—*Jeremiah 17:14 (ERV)*

O LORD my God, I cried to you for help, and you restored my health.
—*Psalm 30:2 (NLT)*

Then a man sick with leprosy came to Jesus. The man bowed down before Jesus and said, "Lord, you have the power to heal me if you want."

Jesus touched the man. Jesus said, "I want to heal you. Be healed!" And immediately the man was healed from his leprosy.
—*Matthew 8:2–3 (ERV)*

When Jesus had entered Capernaum, a centurion came to him, asking for help. "Lord," he said, "my servant lies at home paralyzed and in terrible suffering."

Jesus said to him, "I will go and heal him."

The centurion replied, "Lord, I do not deserve to have you come under my roof. But just say the word, and my servant will be healed. For I myself am a man under authority, with soldiers under me. I tell this one, 'Go,' and he goes; and that one, 'Come,' and he comes. I say to my servant, 'Do this,' and he does it."

When Jesus heard this, he was astonished and said to those following him, "I tell you the truth, I have not found anyone in Israel with such great faith. . . ."

Then Jesus said to the centurion, "Go!

It will be done just as you believed it would." And his servant was healed at that very hour.

—*Matthew 8:5–10, 13 (NIV)*

As Jesus continued on toward Jerusalem, he reached the border between Galilee and Samaria. As he entered a village there, ten lepers stood at a distance, crying out, "Jesus, Master, have mercy on us!"

He looked at them and said, "Go show yourselves to the priests." And as they went, they were cleansed of their leprosy.

One of them, when he saw that he was healed, came back to Jesus, shouting, "Praise God!" He fell to the ground at Jesus' feet, thanking him for what he had done. This man was a Samaritan.

—*Luke 17:11–16 (NLT)*

Do not abandon me, O LORD. Do not stand at a distance, my God. Come quickly to help me, O Lord my savior.
—*Psalm 38:21–22 (NLT)*

Beloved, I pray that you may prosper in all things and be in health, just as your soul prospers.
—*3 John 2 (NKJV)*

Do not be wise in your own eyes; fear the LORD and shun evil. This will bring health to your body and nourishment to your bones.
—*Proverbs 3:7–8 (NIV)*

"But I will restore you to health and heal your wounds," declares the LORD, "because you are called an outcast, Zion for whom no one cares."
—*Jeremiah 30:17 (NIV)*

Simon's mother-in-law was very sick.
She was in bed and had fever. The
people there told Jesus about her. So
Jesus went to her bed. Jesus held her
hand and helped her stand up. The
fever left her, and she was healed. Then
she began serving them.

  —*Mark 1:30–31 (ERV)*

Help AND PROTECTION

Hear my prayer, O LORD, and let my cry come to You. Do not hide Your face from me in the day of my trouble; incline Your ear to me; in the day that I call, answer me speedily.
  —*Psalm 102:1–2 (NKJV)*

God's way is perfect. All the LORD's promises prove true. He is a shield for all who look to him for protection. For who is God except the LORD? Who but our God is a solid rock?
  —*2 Samuel 22:31–32 (NLT)*

Lord, when you do good things to good people, you are like a large shield protecting them.
  —*Psalm 5:12 (ERV)*

In my distress I called upon the LORD, and cried out to my God; He heard my voice from His temple, and my cry came before Him, even to His ears.

—Psalm 18:6 (NKJV)

God's way is perfect. All the LORD's promises prove true. He is a shield for all who look to him for protection.

—Psalm 18:30 (NLT)

I am not asking you to take them out of the world. But I am asking that you keep them safe from the Evil One (the devil).

—John 17:15 (ERV)

The angel of the LORD encamps around those who fear him, and he delivers them.

—Psalm 34:7 (NIV)

Lord, don't leave me! You are my strength. Hurry and help me!

—Psalm 22:19 (ERV)

Cast your burden on the LORD, and He shall sustain you; He shall never permit the righteous to be moved.
—*Psalm 55:22 (NKJV)*

For the LORD gives wisdom, and from his mouth come knowledge and understanding. He holds victory in store for the upright, he is a shield to those whose walk is blameless, for he guards the course of the just and protects the way of his faithful ones.
—*Proverbs 2:6–8 (NIV)*

Those who fear the LORD are secure; he will be a refuge for their children.
—*Proverbs 14:26 (NLT)*

Lord, hear my words. Understand what I am trying to say. My God and King, listen to my prayer.
—*Psalm 5:1–2 (ERV)*

So do not fear, for I am with you; do not be dismayed, for I am your God. I will strengthen you and help you; I will uphold you with my righteous right hand.

—*Isaiah 41:10 (NIV)*

God, you are a hiding place for me. You protect me from my troubles. You surround me and protect me. So I sing about the way you saved me.

—*Psalm 32:7 (ERV)*

So we may boldly say: "The LORD is my helper; I will not fear. What can man do to me?"

—*Hebrews 13:6 (NKJV)*

Do not withhold your mercy from me, O LORD; may your love and your truth always protect me.

—*Psalm 40:11 (NIV)*

The LORD says, "I will rescue those who love me. I will protect those who trust in my name."
—*Psalm 91:14 (NLT)*

The Lord is good. He is a safe place to go to in times of trouble. He takes care of the people who trust him.
—*Nahum 1:7 (ERV)*

Call upon me in the day of trouble; I will deliver you, and you will honor me.
—*Psalm 50:15 (NIV)*

Now she who is really a widow, and left alone, trusts in God and continues in supplications and prayers night and day.
—*1 Timothy 5:5 (NKJV)*

Are you having troubles? You should pray. Are you happy? You should sing.
—*James 5:13 (ERV)*

Keep me safe, O God, for I have come to you for refuge.

— *Psalm 16:1 (NLT)*

"Yes, come," Jesus said.

So Peter went over the side of the boat and walked on the water toward Jesus. But when he saw the strong wind and the waves, he was terrified and began to sink. "Save me, Lord!" he shouted.

Jesus immediately reached out and grabbed him. "You have so little faith," Jesus said. "Why did you doubt me?"

— *Matthew 14:29–31 (NLT)*

Answer me when I call to you, O my righteous God. Give me relief from my distress; be merciful to me and hear my prayer.

— *Psalm 4:1 (NIV)*

Joy AND HOPE

"For I know the plans I have for you,"
says the LORD. "They are plans for
good and not for disaster, to give you a
future and a hope. In those days when
you pray, I will listen. If you look for
me wholeheartedly, you will find me. I
will be found by you," says the LORD. "I
will end your captivity and restore your
fortunes. I will gather you out of the
nations where I sent you and will bring
you home again to your own land."
　　　　—*Jeremiah 29:11–14 (NLT)*

In the same way, the angels of God are
very happy when one sinner changes
his heart.
　　　　—*Luke 15:10 (ERV)*

But let the righteous be glad; let them rejoice before God; yes, let them rejoice exceedingly.

—*Psalm 68:3 (NKJV)*

Let us draw near to God with a sincere heart in full assurance of faith, having our hearts sprinkled to cleanse us from a guilty conscience and having our bodies washed with pure water. Let us hold unswervingly to the hope we profess, for he who promised is faithful.

—*Hebrews 10:22–23 (NIV)*

Everything on earth, shout with joy to God! Praise his glorious name! Honor him with songs of praise! Tell God how wonderful his works are! God, your power is very great! Your enemies bow down. They are afraid of you!

—*Psalm 66:1–3 (ERV)*

Let the righteous rejoice in the LORD and take refuge in him; let all the upright in heart praise him!
    —*Psalm 64:10 (NIV)*

The commandments of the LORD are right, bringing joy to the heart. The commands of the LORD are clear, giving insight for living.
    —*Psalm 19:8 (NLT)*

The LORD is good to those who wait for Him, to the soul who seeks Him. It is good that one should hope and wait quietly for the salvation of the LORD.
    —*Lamentations 3:25–26 (NKJV)*

I pray that the God who gives hope will fill you with much joy and peace while you trust in him. Then you will have more and more hope, and it will flow out of you by the power of the Holy Spirit.
    —*Romans 15:13 (ERV)*

I pray that God will open your minds to see his truth. Then you will know the hope that God has chosen us to have. You will know that the blessings God has promised his holy people are rich and glorious. And you will know that God's power is very great for us who believe. That power is the same as the great strength that God used to raise Christ from death.

—*Ephesians 1:18–20 (ERV)*

We always thank God, the Father of our Lord Jesus Christ, when we pray for you, because we have heard of your faith in Christ Jesus and of the love you have for all the saints—the faith and love that spring from the hope that is stored up for you in heaven and that you have already heard about in the word of truth, the gospel.

—*Colossians 1:3–5 (NIV)*

Why are you downcast, O my soul?
Why so disturbed within me? Put your
hope in God, for I will yet praise him,
my Savior and my God.
                —*Psalm 42:11 (NIV)*

Blessed be the Lord, Who daily loads us
with benefits, the God of our salvation!
                —*Psalm 68:19 (NKJV)*

As for me, I look to the Lord for help.
I wait confidently for God to save me,
and my God will certainly hear me.
                —*Micah 7:7 (NLT)*

Now may our Lord Jesus Christ himself
and God our Father, who loved us and
by his grace gave us eternal comfort
and a wonderful hope, comfort you and
strengthen you in every good thing you
do and say.
                —*2 Thessalonians 2:16–17 (NLT)*

May integrity and uprightness protect me, because my hope is in you.
        —*Psalm 25:21 (NIV)*

Lord, we truly worship you! So show your great love for us.
        —*Psalm 33:22 (ERV)*

Let all that I am wait quietly before God, for my hope is in him.
        —*Psalm 62:5 (NLT)*

Until now you have asked nothing in My name. Ask, and you will receive, that your joy may be full.
        —*John 16:24 (NKJV)*

But I trust in your unfailing love; my heart rejoices in your salvation.
        —*Psalm 13:5 (NIV)*

Therefore, let us offer through Jesus a continual sacrifice of praise to God, proclaiming our allegiance to his name.
        —*Hebrews 13:15 (NLT)*

But let the people who trust God be happy. Let them be happy forever! God, protect and give strength to the people who love your name.

—*Psalm 5:11 (ERV)*

The LORD is my strength and my shield; my heart trusted in Him, and I am helped; therefore my heart greatly rejoices, and with my song I will praise Him.

—*Psalm 28:7 (NKJV)*

Always be joyful.

—*1 Thessalonians 5:16 (NLT)*

Be strong and take heart, all you who hope in the LORD.

—*Psalm 31:24 (NIV)*

Clap your hands, all you nations; shout to God with cries of joy. How awesome is the LORD Most High, the great King over all the earth!

—*Psalm 47:1–2 (NIV)*

God will still fill your mouth with laughter and your lips with happy shouts.

—*Job 8:21 (ERV)*

I know I was ready to fall, but the Lord supported his follower. I was very worried and upset. But Lord, you comforted me and made me happy!

—*Psalm 94:18–19 (ERV)*

Always be full of joy in the Lord. I say it again—rejoice!

—*Philippians 4:4 (NLT)*

You have made known to me the ways of life; You will make me full of joy in Your presence.

—*Acts 2:28 (NKJV)*

Spiritual GROWTH

Ever since I first heard of your strong faith in the Lord Jesus and your love for God's people everywhere, I have not stopped thanking God for you. I pray for you constantly, asking God, the glorious Father of our Lord Jesus Christ, to give you spiritual wisdom and insight so that you might grow in your knowledge of God. I pray that your hearts will be flooded with light so that you can understand the confident hope he has given to those he called— his holy people who are his rich and glorious inheritance. I also pray that you will understand the incredible greatness of God's power for us who believe him. This is the same mighty power.

—*Ephesians 1:15–19 (NLT)*

And may the Lord make you increase and abound in love to one another and to all, just as we do to you, so that He may establish your hearts blameless in holiness before our God and Father at the coming of our Lord Jesus Christ with all His saints.

—*1 Thessalonians 3:12–13 (NKJV)*

And this I pray, that your love may abound still more and more in knowledge and all discernment, that you may approve the things that are excellent, that you may be sincere and without offense till the day of Christ, being filled with the fruits of righteousness which are by Jesus Christ, to the glory and praise of God.

—*Philippians 1:9–11 (NKJV)*

[I am] confident of this, that he who began a good work in you will carry it on to completion until the day of Christ Jesus.

—*Philippians 1:6 (NIV)*

So we have not stopped praying for you since we first heard about you. We ask God to give you complete knowledge of his will and to give you spiritual wisdom and understanding.

—*Colossians 1:9 (NLT)*

We pray that God himself, the God of peace, will make you pure—belonging only to him. We pray that your whole self—spirit, soul, and body—will be kept safe and be without wrong when our Lord Jesus Christ comes.

—*1 Thessalonians 5:23 (ERV)*

With this in mind, we constantly pray for you, that our God may count you worthy of his calling, and that by his power he may fulfill every good purpose of yours and every act prompted by your faith. We pray this so that the name of our Lord Jesus may be glorified in you, and you in him, according to the grace of our God and the Lord Jesus Christ.

—2 Thessalonians 1:11–12 (NIV)

Watch and pray, lest you enter into temptation. The spirit indeed is willing, but the flesh is weak.

—Matthew 26:41 (NKJV)

To reject the law is to praise the wicked; to obey the law is to fight them.

—Proverbs 28:4 (NLT)

Then the way you live will always honor and please the Lord, and your lives will produce every kind of good fruit. All the while, you will grow as you learn to know God better and better. We also pray that you will be strengthened with all his glorious power so you will have all the endurance and patience you need. May you be filled with joy, always thanking the Father. He has enabled you to share in the inheritance that belongs to his people, who live in the light.

—Colossians 1:10–12 (NLT)

No temptation has seized you except what is common to man. And God is faithful; he will not let you be tempted beyond what you can bear. But when you are tempted, he will also provide a way out so that you can stand up under it.

—1 Corinthians 10:13 (NIV)

So set yourselves apart to be holy, for I am the LORD your God. Keep all my decrees by putting them into practice, for I am the LORD who makes you holy.
—*Leviticus 20:7–8 (NLT)*

When a person is being tempted, he should not say, "God is tempting me." Evil cannot tempt God. And God himself does not tempt any person. It is the evil things a person wants that tempt that person. His own evil desire leads him away and holds him.
—*James 1:13–14 (ERV)*

So give yourselves to God. Be against the devil, and the devil will run away from you.
—*James 4:7 (ERV)*

But just as he who called you is holy, so be holy in all you do; for it is written: "Be holy, because I am holy."
—*1 Peter 1:15–16 (NIV)*

Create in me a clean heart, O God. Renew a loyal spirit within me.
—*Psalm 51:10 (NLT)*

For we do not have a High Priest who cannot sympathize with our weaknesses, but was in all points tempted as we are, yet without sin.
—*Hebrews 4:15 (NKJV)*

O LORD, be gracious to us; we long for you. Be our strength every morning, our salvation in time of distress.
—*Isaiah 33:2 (NIV)*

God is my strength and power, and He makes my way perfect. He makes my feet like the feet of deer, and sets me on my high places.
—*2 Samuel 22:33–34 (NKJV)*

The LORD gives his people strength. The LORD blesses them with peace.
—*Psalm 29:11 (NLT)*

Do you not know? Have you not heard? The LORD is the everlasting God, the Creator of the ends of the earth. He will not grow tired or weary, and his understanding no one can fathom. He gives strength to the weary and increases the power of the weak. Even youths grow tired and weary, and young men stumble and fall; but those who hope in the LORD will renew their strength. They will soar on wings like eagles; they will run and not grow weary, they will walk and not be faint.

—*Isaiah 40:28–31 (NIV)*

My health may fail, and my spirit may grow weak, but God remains the strength of my heart; he is mine forever.

—*Psalm 73:26 (NLT)*

Look to the Lord and his strength. Always go to him for help.

—*1 Chronicles 16:11 (ERV)*

I love you, LORD; you are my strength.
The LORD is my rock, my fortress, and
my savior; my God is my rock, in whom
I find protection. He is my shield, the
power that saves me, and my place of
safety.

—*Psalm 18:1–2 (NLT)*

[I pray] that He would grant you,
according to the riches of His glory, to
be strengthened with might through His
Spirit in the inner man.

—*Ephesians 3:16 (NKJV)*

The LORD is my strength and my shield;
my heart trusts in him, and I am
helped. My heart leaps for joy and I will
give thanks to him in song. The LORD is
the strength of his people, a fortress of
salvation for his anointed one.

—*Psalm 28:7–8 (NIV)*

Wisdom AND GUIDANCE

That night God appeared to Solomon and said to him, "Ask for whatever you want me to give you."

Solomon answered God, "You have shown great kindness to David my father and have made me king in his place. Now, LORD God, let your promise to my father David be confirmed, for you have made me king over a people who are as numerous as the dust of the earth. Give me wisdom and knowledge, that I may lead this people, for who is able to govern this great people of yours?"

God said to Solomon, "Since this is your heart's desire and you have not asked for wealth, riches or honor, nor for the death of your enemies, and since you have not asked for a long life but

for wisdom and knowledge to govern my people over whom I have made you king, therefore wisdom and knowledge will be given you. And I will also give you wealth, riches and honor, such as no king who was before you ever had and none after you will have."
—2 Chronicles 1:7–12 (NIV)

In the same way, wisdom is good for your soul. If you have wisdom, then you will have hope, and your hope will never end.
—Proverbs 24:14 (ERV)

If any of you lacks wisdom, he should ask God, who gives generously to all without finding fault, and it will be given to him.
—James 1:5 (NIV)

But you desire honesty from the womb, teaching me wisdom even there.
—Psalm 51:6 (NLT)

Now therefore, I pray, if I have found grace in Your sight, show me now Your way, that I may know You and that I may find grace in Your sight. And consider that this nation is Your people.
—*Exodus 33:13 (NKJV)*

Lead me, O LORD, in your righteousness because of my enemies— make straight your way before me.
—*Psalm 5:8 (NIV)*

But the Helper will teach you everything. The Helper will cause you to remember all the things I told you. This Helper is the Holy Spirit that the Father will send in my name.
—*John 14:26 (ERV)*

You will show me the way of life, granting me the joy of your presence and the pleasures of living with you forever.
—*Psalm 16:11 (NLT)*

For this God is our God for ever and ever; he will be our guide even to the end.

  —*Psalm 48:14 (NIV)*

Your Spirit is in every place I go. Lord, I can't escape you. Lord, if I go up to heaven, you are there. If I go down to the place of death, you are there. Lord, if I go east where the sun rises, you are there. If I go west to the sea, you are there. Even there your right hand holds me, and you lead me by the hand.

  —*Psalm 139:7–10 (ERV)*

Trust the Lord completely! Don't depend on your own knowledge. Think about God in all that you do. Then he will help you.

  —*Proverbs 3:5–6 (ERV)*

I will bring the blind by a way they did not know; I will lead them in paths they have not known. I will make darkness light before them, and crooked places straight. These things I will do for them, and not forsake them.

—*Isaiah 42:16 (NKJV)*

Guide me in your truth and teach me, for you are God my Savior, and my hope is in you all day long. . . . Good and upright is the LORD; therefore he instructs sinners in his ways. He guides the humble in what is right and teaches them his way.

—*Psalm 25:5, 8–9 (NIV)*

Judah, pray to me, and I will answer you. I will tell you important secrets. You have never heard these things before.

—*Jeremiah 33:3 (ERV)*

But when he, the Spirit of truth, comes, he will guide you into all truth. He will not speak on his own; he will speak only what he hears, and he will tell you what is yet to come.

—*John 16:13 (NIV)*

The LORD will guide you continually, giving you water when you are dry and restoring your strength. You will be like a well-watered garden, like an ever-flowing spring.

—*Isaiah 58:11 (NLT)*

God, let your light and truth shine on me. Your light and truth will guide me. They will lead me to your holy mountain. They will lead me to your home.

—*Psalm 43:3 (ERV)*

The Lord gives wisdom. Knowledge and understanding come from his mouth.

—*Proverbs 2:6 (ERV)*

Daniel answered and said: "Blessed be the name of God forever and ever, for wisdom and might are His. And He changes the times and the seasons; He removes kings and raises up kings; He gives wisdom to the wise and knowledge to those who have understanding."

—*Daniel 2:20–21 (NKJV)*

Thus says the LORD: "Stand in the ways and see, and ask for the old paths, where the good way is, and walk in it; then you will find rest for your souls. But they said, 'We will not walk in it.'"

—*Jeremiah 6:16 (NKJV)*

The law of the LORD is perfect, reviving the soul. The statutes of the LORD are trustworthy, making wise the simple.

—*Psalm 19:7 (NIV)*

God, you are my Rock, so, for the good of your name, lead me and guide me.

—*Psalm 31:3 (ERV)*

Fear of the LORD is the foundation of true wisdom. All who obey his commandments will grow in wisdom. Praise him forever!
—*Psalm 111:10 (NLT)*

You, through Your commandments, make me wiser than my enemies; for they are ever with me.
—*Psalm 119:98 (NKJV)*

Get wisdom and understanding! Don't forget my words. Always follow my teachings. Don't turn away from wisdom. Then wisdom will protect you. Love wisdom, and wisdom will keep you safe. Wisdom begins when you decide to get wisdom. So use everything you own to get wisdom! Then you will become wise.
—*Proverbs 4:5–7 (ERV)*

How much better to get wisdom than gold, to choose understanding rather than silver!

—*Proverbs 16:16 (NIV)*

Buy the truth, and do not sell it, also wisdom and instruction and understanding.

—*Proverbs 23:23 (NKJV)*

But the wisdom from above is first of all pure. It is also peace loving, gentle at all times, and willing to yield to others. It is full of mercy and good deeds. It shows no favoritism and is always sincere.

—*James 3:17 (NLT)*

Prayer

TOUCHES OTHERS

But I tell you, love your enemies.
Pray for those people that do bad
things to you.

—Matthew 5:44 (ERV)

Family AND FRIENDS

And be kind to one another,
tenderhearted, forgiving one another,
even as God in Christ forgave you.
—*Ephesians 4:32 (NKJV)*

Suppose a person sees his brother or
sister in Christ sinning (sin that does
not lead to eternal death). That person
should pray for his brother or sister
who is sinning. Then God will give
the brother or sister life. I am talking
about people whose sin does not lead
to eternal death. There is sin that leads
to death. I don't mean that a person
should pray about that sin.
—*1 John 5:16 (ERV)*

Every time I think of you, I give thanks to my God.
> —*Philippians 1:3 (NLT)*

I thank my God, making mention of you always in my prayers, hearing of your love and faith which you have toward the Lord Jesus and toward all the saints, that the sharing of your faith may become effective by the acknowledgment of every good thing which is in you in Christ Jesus.
> —*Philemon 4–6 (NKJV)*

May God give you of heaven's dew and of earth's richness—an abundance of grain and new wine. May nations serve you and peoples bow down to you. Be lord over your brothers, and may the sons of your mother bow down to you. May those who curse you be cursed and those who bless you be blessed.
> —*Genesis 27:28–29 (NIV)*

Always tell each other the wrong things you have done. Then pray for each other. Do this so that God can heal you. When a good person prays hard, great things happen.

　　　—*James 5:16 (ERV)*

Isaac prayed to the LORD on behalf of his wife, because she was barren. The LORD answered his prayer, and his wife Rebekah became pregnant.

　　　—*Genesis 25:21 (NIV)*

May the LORD richly bless both you and your children. May you be blessed by the LORD, who made heaven and earth.

　　　—*Psalm 115:14–15 (NLT)*

Pray for us. We are sure that we have a clear conscience and desire to live honorably in every way.

　　　—*Hebrews 13:18 (NIV)*

I urge you, first of all, to pray for all people. Ask God to help them; intercede on their behalf, and give thanks for them.

—*1 Timothy 2:1 (NLT)*

I want men everywhere to lift up holy hands in prayer, without anger or disputing.

—*1 Timothy 2:8 (NIV)*

It will be very bad for King Jehoiakim. He is doing bad things so he can build his palace. He is cheating people so he can build rooms upstairs. He is making his own people work for nothing. He is not paying them for their work.

—*Jeremiah 22:13 (ERV)*

May the LORD bless you and protect you. May the LORD smile on you and be gracious to you. May the LORD show you his favor and give you his peace.
—*Numbers 6:24–26 (NLT)*

Do not be a witness against your neighbor without cause, for would you deceive with your lips?
—*Proverbs 24:28 (NKJV)*

For the commandments, "You shall not commit adultery," "You shall not murder," "You shall not steal," "You shall not bear false witness," "You shall not covet," and if there is any other commandment, are all summed up in this saying, namely, "You shall love your neighbor as yourself." Love does no harm to a neighbor; therefore love is the fulfillment of the law.
—*Romans 13:9–10 (NKJV)*

When Jesus had finished saying all this to the people, he returned to Capernaum. At that time the highly valued slave of a Roman officer was sick and near death. When the officer heard about Jesus, he sent some respected Jewish elders to ask him to come and heal his slave. So they earnestly begged Jesus to help the man. "If anyone deserves your help, he does," they said, "for he loves the Jewish people and even built a synagogue for us."

So Jesus went with them. But just before they arrived at the house, the officer sent some friends to say, "Lord, don't trouble yourself by coming to my home, for I am not worthy of such an honor. I am not even worthy to come and meet you. Just say the word from where you are, and my servant will be healed. I know this because I am under the authority of my superior officers, and I have authority over my soldiers. I only need to say, 'Go,' and they go, or 'Come,' and they come. And if I say to my slaves, 'Do this,' they do it."

When Jesus heard this, he was amazed. Turning to the crowd that was following him, he said, "I tell you, I haven't seen faith like this in all Israel!" And when the officer's friends returned to his house, they found the slave completely healed.

—*Luke 7:1–10 (NLT)*

Do not seek revenge or bear a grudge against one of your people, but love your neighbor as yourself. I am the LORD.

—*Leviticus 19:18 (NIV)*

We should help others do what is right and build them up in the Lord.

—*Romans 15:2 (NLT)*

Jesus said to his followers, "There are many, many people to harvest (save). But there are only a few workers to help harvest them. God owns the harvest (people). Pray to him that he will send more workers to help gather his harvest."
—*Matthew 9:37–38 (ERV)*

Pray also for me, that whenever I open my mouth, words may be given me so that I will fearlessly make known the mystery of the gospel, for which I am an ambassador in chains. Pray that I may declare it fearlessly, as I should.
—*Ephesians 6:19–20 (NIV)*

For all the law is fulfilled in one word, even in this: "You shall love your neighbor as yourself."
—*Galatians 5:14 (NKJV)*

Enemies

I say to you people that are listening to me, love your enemies. Do good to those people that hate you. Ask God to bless those people that say bad things to you. Pray for those people that are mean to you. If a person hits you on the side of your face, let him hit the other side too. If a person takes your coat, don't stop him from taking your shirt too. Give to every person that asks you. When a person takes something that is yours, don't ask for it back. Do for other people what you want them to do for you.

—Luke 6:27–31 (ERV)

But I tell you, love your enemies. Pray
for those people that do bad things to
you.
     —Matthew 5:44 (ERV)

If you love only those who love you,
why should you get credit for that?
Even sinners love those who love them!
And if you do good only to those who do
good to you, why should you get credit?
Even sinners do that much! And if
you lend money only to those who can
repay you, why should you get credit?
Even sinners will lend to other sinners
for a full return. Love your enemies!
Do good to them. Lend to them without
expecting to be repaid. Then your
reward from heaven will be very great,
and you will truly be acting as children
of the Most High, for he is kind to those
who are unthankful and wicked.
     —Luke 6:32–35 (NLT)

When they came to a place called The Skull, they nailed him to the cross. And the criminals were also crucified—one on his right and one on his left. Jesus said, "Father, forgive them, for they don't know what they are doing." And the soldiers gambled for his clothes by throwing dice.

—Luke 23:33–34 (NLT)

THE HEARTFELT

Prayers

OF . . .

I keep asking that the God of our Lord Jesus Christ, the glorious Father, may give you the Spirit of wisdom and revelation, so that you may know him better.

—Ephesians 1:17 (NIV)

Abraham's SERVANT

Then he prayed, "O LORD, God of my master Abraham, give me success today, and show kindness to my master Abraham. See, I am standing beside this spring, and the daughters of the townspeople are coming out to draw water. May it be that when I say to a girl, 'Please let down your jar that I may have a drink,' and she says, 'Drink, and I'll water your camels too'—let her be the one you have chosen for your servant Isaac. By this I will know that you have shown kindness to my master."

Before he had finished praying, Rebekah came out with her jar on her shoulder. She was the daughter of Bethuel son of Milcah, who was the wife of Abraham's brother Nahor. The girl was very beautiful, a virgin; no man had ever lain with her. She went down to the spring, filled her jar and came up again.

The servant hurried to meet her and said, "Please give me a little water from your jar."

"Drink, my lord," she said, and quickly lowered the jar to her hands and gave him a drink.

After she had given him a drink, she said, "I'll draw water for your camels too, until they have finished drinking." So she quickly emptied her jar into the trough, ran back to the well to draw more water, and drew enough for all his camels. . . . Then the man bowed down and worshiped the LORD, saying, "Praise be to the LORD, the God of my master Abraham, who has not abandoned his kindness and faithfulness to my master. As for me, the LORD has led me on the journey to the house of my master's relatives."

—*Genesis 24:12–20, 26–27 (NIV)*

Hannah

After eating and drinking, Hannah quietly got up and went to pray to the Lord. Eli the priest was sitting on a chair near the door of the Lord's Holy Building. Hannah was very sad. She cried very much while she prayed to the Lord. She made a special promise to God. She said, "Lord All-Powerful, see how very sad I am. Remember me! Don't forget me. If you will give me a son, then I will give him to you. He will be a Nazirite: He will not drink wine or strong drink. And no one will ever cut his hair."

Hannah prayed to the Lord a long time. Eli was watching Hannah's mouth while she was praying. Hannah was praying in her heart. Her lips were moving, but she did not say the words out loud. So Eli thought Hannah was drunk. Eli said to Hannah, "You have had too much to drink! It is time to put away the wine."

Hannah answered, "Sir, I have not drunk any wine or beer. I am deeply troubled. I was telling the Lord about all my problems. Don't think I am a bad woman. I have been praying so long because I have so many troubles and I am very sad."

Eli answered, "Go in peace. May the God of Israel give you the things you asked."

Hannah said, "I hope you are happy with me." Then Hannah left and ate something. She was not sad any more.

Early the next morning Elkanah's family got up. They worshiped the Lord and then went back home to Ramah.

Elkanah had sexual relations with his wife Hannah, and the Lord remembered

Hannah. By that time the following year, Hannah had become pregnant and had a son. Hannah named her son Samuel. She said, "His name is Samuel because I asked the Lord for him."

—*1 Samuel 1:9–20 (ERV)*

David

Lord, you tested me. You know all
about me. You know when I sit down
and when I get up. You know my
thoughts from far away. Lord, you know
where I am going and when I am lying
down. You know everything I do. Lord,
you know what I want to say, even
before the words leave my mouth. Lord,
you are all around me—in front and in
back of me. You gently put your hand
on me. I am amazed at what you know.
It is too much for me to understand.
Your Spirit is in every place I go. Lord,
I can't escape you. Lord, if I go up to
heaven, you are there. If I go down to
the place of death, you are there. Lord,
if I go east where the sun rises, you are
there. If I go west to the sea, you are

there. Even there your right hand holds me, and you lead me by the hand.

Lord, I might try to hide from you and say, "The day has changed to night. Surely the darkness will hide me." But even darkness is not dark to you, Lord, the night is as bright as day to you. Lord, you made my whole body. You knew all about me while I was still in my mother's body. Lord, I praise you! You made me in an amazing and wonderful way. I know very well that what you did is wonderful!

You know all about me. You watched my bones grow while my body took shape, hidden in my mother's body. You watched my body parts grow. You listed them all in your book. You watched me every day. Not one of them is missing. Your thoughts are important

to me. God, you know so much! If I could count them, they would be more than all the grains of sand. And when I finished, I would still be with you.
—*Psalm 139:1–18 (ERV)*

Solomon

At Gibeon the LORD appeared to
Solomon in a dream by night; and God
said, "Ask! What shall I give you?" And
Solomon said: "You have shown great
mercy to Your servant David my father,
because he walked before You in truth,
in righteousness, and in uprightness of
heart with You; You have continued this
great kindness for him, and You have
given him a son to sit on his throne, as
it is this day. Now, O LORD my God, You
have made Your servant king instead of
my father David, but I am a little child;
I do not know how to go out or come
in. And Your servant is in the midst of
Your people whom You have chosen,
a great people, too numerous to be
numbered or counted. Therefore give to
Your servant an understanding heart to

judge Your people, that I may discern between good and evil. For who is able to judge this great people of Yours?"

The speech pleased the Lord, that Solomon had asked this thing. Then God said to him: "Because you have asked this thing, and have not asked long life for yourself, nor have asked riches for yourself, nor have asked the life of your enemies, but have asked for yourself understanding to discern justice, behold, I have done according to your words; see, I have given you a wise and understanding heart, so that there has not been anyone like you before you, nor shall any like you arise after you. And I have also given you what you have not asked: both riches and honor, so that there shall not be anyone like you among the kings all your days. So if you walk in My ways, to keep My statutes and My commandments, as your father David walked, then I will lengthen your days." Then Solomon awoke; and indeed it had been a dream. And he came to Jerusalem and stood before the ark of the covenant of the LORD, offered up burnt offerings, offered peace offerings, and made a feast for all his servants.

—*1 Kings 3:5–15 (NKJV)*

Jehoshaphat

Jehoshaphat was in the Lord's temple
in front of the new yard. He stood up in
the meeting of the people from Judah
and Jerusalem. He said, "Lord God
of our ancestors, you are the God in
heaven! You rule over all the kingdoms
in all the nations! You have power and
strength! No person can stand against
you! You are our God! You forced the
people living in this land to leave. You
did this in front of your people Israel.
You gave this land to the descendants
of Abraham forever. Abraham was
your friend. Abraham's descendants
lived in this land, and built a temple
for your name. They said, 'If trouble
comes to us—the sword, punishment,
sicknesses, or famine, we will stand in

front of this temple and in front of you. Your name is on this temple. We will shout to you when we are in trouble. Then you will hear and save us.'

"But now, here are men from Ammon, Moab, and Mount Seir! You would not let the people of Israel enter their lands when the people of Israel came out of Egypt. So the people of Israel turned away and didn't destroy those people. But see the kind of reward those people give us for not destroying them. They have come to force us out of your land. You gave this land to us. Our God, punish those people! We have no power against this large army that is coming against us! We don't know what to do! That is why we look to you for help!"

—*2 Chronicles 20:5–12 (ERV)*

Hezekiah

And Hezekiah prayed to the LORD: "O LORD, God of Israel, enthroned between the cherubim, you alone are God over all the kingdoms of the earth. You have made heaven and earth. Give ear, O LORD, and hear; open your eyes, O LORD, and see; listen to the words Sennacherib has sent to insult the living God.

"It is true, O LORD, that the Assyrian kings have laid waste these nations and their lands. They have thrown their gods into the fire and destroyed them, for they were not gods but only wood and stone, fashioned by men's hands. Now, O LORD our God, deliver us from his hand, so that all kingdoms on earth may know that you alone, O LORD, are God."

—2 Kings 19:15–19 (NIV)

About that time Hezekiah became deathly ill, and the prophet Isaiah son of Amoz went to visit him. He gave the king this message: "This is what the LORD says: Set your affairs in order, for you are going to die. You will not recover from this illness."

When Hezekiah heard this, he turned his face to the wall and prayed to the LORD, "Remember, O LORD, how I have always been faithful to you and have served you single-mindedly, always doing what pleases you." Then he broke down and wept bitterly.

But before Isaiah had left the middle courtyard, this message came to him from the LORD: "Go back to Hezekiah, the leader of my people. Tell him, 'This is what the LORD, the God of your ancestor David, says: I have heard your prayer and seen your tears. I will heal you, and three days from now you will get out of bed and go to the Temple of the LORD. I will add fifteen years to your life, and I will rescue you and this city from the king of Assyria. I will defend this city for my own honor and for the sake of my servant David.'"

Then Isaiah said, "Make an ointment from figs." So Hezekiah's servants spread the ointment over the boil, and Hezekiah recovered!

—*2 Kings 20:1–7 (NLT)*

Daniel

Then the secret was revealed to Daniel in a night vision. So Daniel blessed the God of heaven. Daniel answered and said: "Blessed be the name of God forever and ever, for wisdom and might are His. And He changes the times and the seasons; He removes kings and raises up kings; He gives wisdom to the wise and knowledge to those who have understanding. He reveals deep and secret things; He knows what is in the darkness, and light dwells with Him. I thank You and praise You, O God of my fathers; You have given me wisdom and might, and have now made known to me what we asked of You, for You have made known to us the king's demand."

—Daniel 2:19–23 (NKJV)

Habakkuk

I have heard all about you, LORD. I am filled with awe by your amazing works. In this time of our deep need, help us again as you did in years gone by. And in your anger, remember your mercy....

When he stops, the earth shakes. When he looks, the nations tremble. He shatters the everlasting mountains and levels the eternal hills. He is the Eternal One! . . .

The sun and moon stood still in the sky as your brilliant arrows flew and your glittering spear flashed.

You marched across the land in anger and trampled the nations in your fury. You went out to rescue your chosen people, to save your anointed ones. You crushed the heads of the wicked and stripped their bones from head to toe.

With his own weapons, you destroyed
the chief of those who rushed out like
a whirlwind, thinking Israel would be
easy prey. You trampled the sea with
your horses, and the mighty waters
piled high.

I trembled inside when I heard this;
my lips quivered with fear. My legs gave
way beneath me, and I shook in terror.
I will wait quietly for the coming day
when disaster will strike the people who
invade us. Even though the fig trees
have no blossoms, and there are no
grapes on the vines; even though the
olive crop fails, and the fields lie empty
and barren; even though the flocks die
in the fields, and the cattle barns are
empty, yet I will rejoice in the LORD! I
will be joyful in the God of my salvation!
The Sovereign LORD is my strength! He
makes me as surefooted as a deer, able
to tread upon the heights.

—*Habakkuk 3:2, 6, 11–19 (NLT)*

Zechariah

His father Zechariah was filled with the Holy Spirit and prophesied: "Praise be to the Lord, the God of Israel, because he has come and has redeemed his people. He has raised up a horn of salvation for us in the house of his servant David (as he said through his holy prophets of long ago), salvation from our enemies and from the hand of all who hate us—to show mercy to our fathers and to remember his holy covenant, the oath he swore to our father Abraham: to rescue us from the hand of our enemies, and to enable us to serve him without fear in holiness and righteousness before him all our days. And you, my child, will be called a prophet of the Most High; for you will go on before the Lord to prepare

the way for him, to give his people the
knowledge of salvation through the
forgiveness of their sins, because of the
tender mercy of our God, by which the
rising sun will come to us from heaven
to shine on those living in darkness and
in the shadow of death, to guide our
feet into the path of peace."

—Luke 1:67–79 (NIV)

Mary

And Mary said: "My soul magnifies
the Lord, and my spirit has rejoiced in
God my Savior. For He has regarded
the lowly state of His maidservant; for
behold, henceforth all generations will
call me blessed. For He who is mighty
has done great things for me, and
holy is His name. And His mercy is on
those who fear Him from generation to
generation. He has shown strength with
His arm; He has scattered the proud
in the imagination of their hearts. He
has put down the mighty from their
thrones, and exalted the lowly. He has
filled the hungry with good things,
and the rich He has sent away empty.
He has helped His servant Israel, in
remembrance of His mercy, as He
spoke to our fathers, to Abraham and
to his seed forever."

—Luke 1:46–55 (NKJV)

Jesus

So when you pray, you should pray like this: "Our Father in heaven, we pray that your name will always be kept holy. We pray that your kingdom will come, and that the things you want will be done here on earth, the same as in heaven. Give us the food we need for each day. Forgive the sins we have done, the same as we have forgiven the people that did wrong to us. Don't let us be tempted (tested); but save us from the Evil One (the devil)."

—*Matthew 6:9–13 (ERV)*

Paul

This letter is from Paul, chosen by the will of God to be an apostle of Christ Jesus. I am writing to God's holy people in Ephesus, who are faithful followers of Christ Jesus. . . .

I have not stopped thanking God for you. I pray for you constantly, asking God, the glorious Father of our Lord Jesus Christ, to give you spiritual wisdom and insight so that you might grow in your knowledge of God. I pray that your hearts will be flooded with light so that you can understand the confident hope he has given to those he called—his holy people who are his rich and glorious inheritance.

I also pray that you will understand the incredible greatness of God's power for us who believe him. This is the same mighty power

—*Ephesians 1:1, 16–19 (NLT)*

 *Other* TITLES TO ENJOY IN THIS SERIES INCLUDE: